FACEBOOK
Keeping You Secure

David Lyon

Contents

Introduction

My name is David Lyon and I am a security professional. I am a Certified Information Systems Security Professional and have been working professionally in the information technology (IT) field for more than 10 years. My professional experience has included healthcare, education, Department of Defense contractors and even a two-employee business. I have always been the 'go-to' person for all things technology and security with my friends, family and coworkers. While not working, I enjoy tinkering with my various cars, doing home improvement projects and trying out new recipes for different types of food.

I promise to give you the honest facts about your security online and on Facebook. You may not agree with everything I say, and that's OK. I provide you information based on my experience, research and knowledge of the IT and cyber security world.

Please let me know if you find any errors or have any comments on the topic of this book.

Piracy

While I would hope everyone who reads this book has purchased it legitimately, I know that's far from reality. If you have downloaded a copy of this book from somewhere besides Amazon, all I ask is you review the book. Please write your review on either Amazon or Goodreads to help others find my books.

Standards and Notes

While writing this book, there are several standards I like to follow for formatting.

Complicated links are shortened using Google's goo.gl link creator. This will ease visiting the links mentioned. I know it can be tough to follow links from an eBook or paper copy, but these shortened links should help. They are case sensitive and will be followed by a description of where the link will take you (e.g. Amazon.com).

To draw more attention to certain items, I will use the following icons.

 Information to take note of is designated with this pencil icon.

 When some information or action requires more caution, this icon will be used.

 This icon will allow you to further explore the topic covered with sources and search terms.

Facebook and Security

Facebook is the most popular social media network on the Internet with more than 1.1 billion daily users as of June 2016. This popularity paints Facebook as a target for hackers and deviants. Your account is the primary target of these Facebook hacks.

Why is your account important? It contains a wealth of information on your personal life and can be used to send viruses or spy on you and your friends. Information gathered from an active Facebook account can be used to crack passwords for other online accounts or answer security questions at banks.

Statistics for compromised accounts are not widely published, but this news report in 2011 claims some 600,000 accounts are compromised every day. https://goo.gl/qVEYuV (NYDailyNews.com).

A more recent news article (2015) puts the number at 160,000 accounts hacked per day. https://goo.gl/EgYypw (NYPost.com).

The truth may lie somewhere in the middle, but either number is staggering.

My goal is to keep you from being the next victim. We will work to lock down your account and then ensure your information is only visible to a specific list of friends you choose.

Throughout this book, we will require the use of a web browser to visit www.Facebook.com on a desktop or laptop computer. The menu options within the Facebook app on iPhones and Android devices are similar to the Facebook website, but no screen shots are provided for mobile devices.

Account Security

Our first mission for Facebook security is to secure your account. We want to make sure you are the only person who can log in. Using your laptop or desktop computer, open your favorite web browser and navigate to www. Facebook.com and login. After you have reached the main page, click on the down arrow, next to the question mark icon, in the top right. Then click *Settings*. This menu is where we will be spending most of our time to update your security settings.

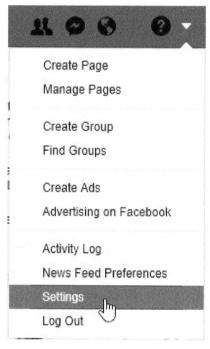

The next screen is the *Privacy Settings and Tools,* click on *Security* on the left column.

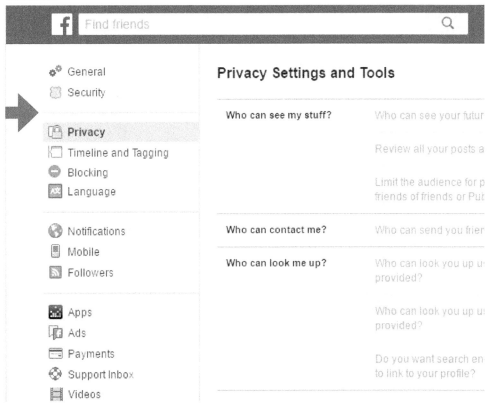

A majority of this chapter will be focused on this screen and these settings. These security settings are where we will keep hackers out of your Facebook account. Throughout this section, you may be asked for your password to change these settings.

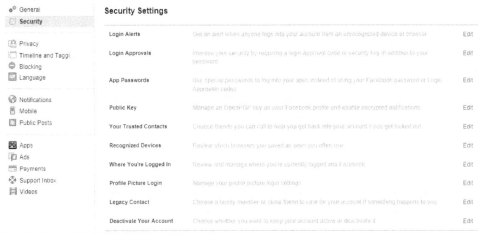

Here is a close up of the options on the page. Each has a brief description to the right. We'll go through each option next. Changing options on this page will require you to reenter your password.

Security Settings

Login Alerts

Login Approvals

App Passwords

Public Key

Your Trusted Contacts

Recognized Devices

Where You're Logged In

Profile Picture Login

Legacy Contact

Deactivate Your Account

Login Alerts

To prevent someone from logging in to your Facebook account from an unknown device, set up Login Alerts. With this option enabled, you receive a notification when someone logs in to your account from an unknown device. Unknown devices could be a tablet, smart phone or computer that you have never used to log in to your Facebook account previously. These alerts can be Facebook notifications, an email sent to your addresses on your account or text message delivered to your cell phone.

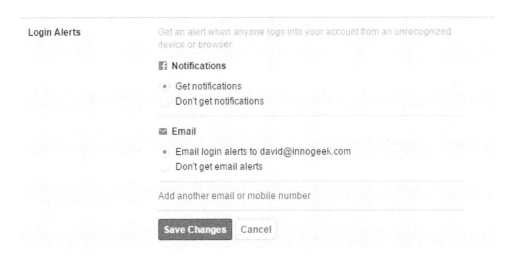

Recommendation: Enable both the notifications and email/text message notification and click *Save Changes*. These notifications would alert you the minute your account is compromised.

Login Approvals

When logging in to your Facebook account from a new device, enabling Login Approvals will require another form of authentication. Facebook allows you to pick from a code generated by the Facebook App, receiving a text message, having a security key or printing recovery codes. This is a security practice called Two-Factor Authentication. By requiring you to enter a code from one of these methods, Facebook confirms you not only know your password, but also have and can access your secondary codes. Enable as many options as you'd like, you are only required to use one of these methods when logging in. For example, if you have your phone, but not your code generator, you can select to receive a *Text Message* instead of using the *Code Generator.*

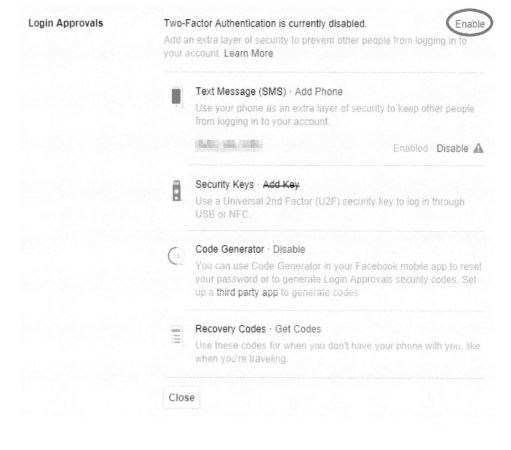

Recommendation: Enable this security setting to keep the bad guys out. This security feature enables Multifactor Authentication, which makes your account significantly harder to hack. Your password alone will not grant access to your Facebook account.

Click *Enable* in the top right of this section.

Facebook will prompt you with the above screen shot. My recommendation is to uncheck the box immediately enabling Two-Factor Authentication. Click *Enable*.

Turn On Login Approvals?

Are you sure you want to enable Two-Factor Authentication?

✓ For the next seven days, do not require a second factor to disable Login Approvals.

Cancel   Enable

The prompt above will appear if you unchecked the box on the last screen. Click *Close*.

Login Approvals Enabled

You must now use a code or security key in order to log in to unrecognized devices.

Close

Now that Login Approvals have been activated, it's time to add some devices to receive codes. The first option is to add a phone to receive text messages.

 Text Message (SMS)
Use your phone as an extra layer of security to keep other people from logging in to your account.

If you already have a cell phone linked to your Facebook account, the option will look like the screenshot below. Since the Text Message option is *Enabled* there would be nothing to turn on. We're going to assume you do not have a phone linked to your account.

 Text Message (SMS) · Add Phone
Use your phone as an extra layer of security to keep other people from logging in to your account.

   Enabled · Disable

Click *Add Phone.*

Enter your phone number, with area code, in the middle box. Click *Continue*. Facebook will immediately send you a text message code to confirm your number.

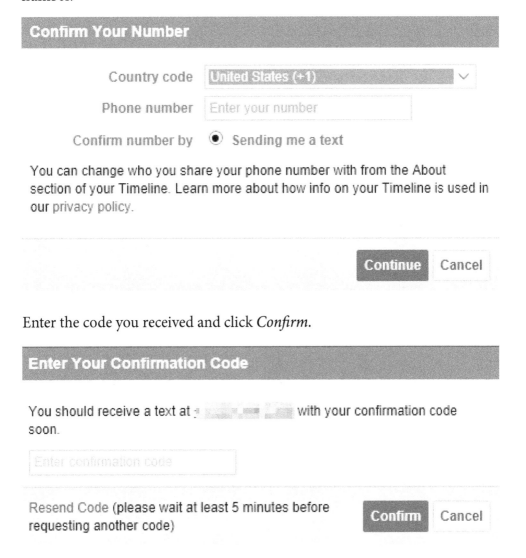

Enter the code you received and click *Confirm*.

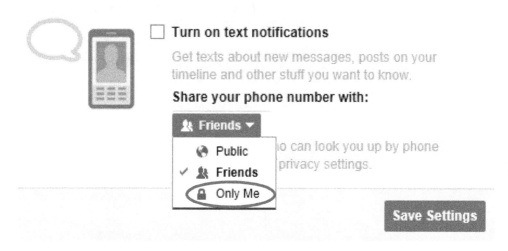

Facebook now asks whether you would like text notifications about new messages and posts. I would advise against this depending on how active you are on Facebook. It also asks with whom you would like to share your phone number. My recommendation is *Only Me* to protect your phone number.

The next section is *Security Keys. Security Keys* are USB dongles, which you would be required to plug in to the computer you are using to access your account. The recommended *Security Keys* are approximately $40 on Amazon and their configuration is beyond the scope of this book. If you have a key, click *Add Key* and follow the steps provided.

Next is *Code Generator*. It is my recommendation to enable this feature. There are two ways to enable this feature. First would be to use Facebook's built in code generator and the second would be using a third party application to generator the codes like Google Authenticator or Authy. Both options require a smart phone and the first option requires you have the Facebook App installed.

To use the Facebook Code Generator, click *Setup*.

 Code Generator (Setup)
You can use Code Generator in your Facebook mobile app to reset your password or to generate Login Approvals security codes. Set up a third party app to generate codes

Follow the directions above within the Facebook App on your smart phone. Click *Continue*.

Turn on Security Codes   ✕

Activate Code Generator to get security codes on your phone. [?]

1. Open the Facebook app on your phone
2. Tap the menu button
3. Scroll down and tap **Code Generator**
4. Tap **Activate**

When Code Generator is activated, click **Continue**.

Having trouble?   Cancel   **Continue**

Test Code Generator

✕

You have to follow the steps in the previous page and click **Activate** to use the Code Generator.

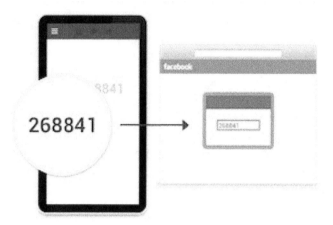

To test Code Generator, enter the security code that appears on your phone.

Back   Enable Two-Factor Authentication

Enter the code displayed on your phone in the box above and then click *Enable Two-Factor Authentication.*

If this is the first Two-Factor Authentication method added to your account, you may be asked the above question. I recommend unchecking the box and clicking *Enable.*

Turn On Login Approvals?

Are you sure you want to enable Two-Factor Authentication?

For the next seven days, do not require a second factor to disable Login Approvals.

Cancel   **Enable**

If you would rather use a third party application like Google Authenticator or Authy, click on *third party app.*

Code Generator · Setup

You can use Code Generator in your Facebook mobile app to reset your password or to generate Login Approvals security codes. Set up a **third party app** to generate codes

Facebook will provide you a QR code (square bar code) and Secret key. Use your chosen application to either scan or enter the key. I recommend using Google Authenticator.

Google Authenticator will then generate a code. Enter it in the *Security Code* box above and click *Confirm. Code Generator* is now enabled on your account.

Set Up a Third Party App to Generate Codes

To get a third party app working, either scan the QR code below or type the secret key into the app.

QR code:

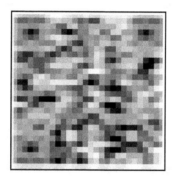

Secret key:

To confirm the third party app is set up correctly, enter the security code that appears on your phone.

Security code:

Cancel   Confirm

The final section is *Recovery Codes,* which are good when traveling or your phone is unavailable.

Click *Get Codes.* You are provided 10 codes, which you can print and store somewhere safe.

 Recovery Codes (Get Codes)
Use these codes for when you don't have your phone with you, like when you're traveling.

Click *Print Codes.* Each code is single use; if you run out of codes, come back to this page and click *get new codes.*

Your Login Approvals Codes

Use these codes for Login Approvals when you don't have your phone with you, like when you're traveling.

You still have **10** codes available. Print them out, keep them safe and use them whenever a Login Approvals code is required to log in.

You can get new codes if you're running low, just remember only the newest set of codes will work.

Close   **Print Codes**

Another benefit of recovery codes is they will allow you to login if you no longer have access to your phone and code generator. Print them and keep them somewhere safe.

App Passwords

After enabling *Login Approvals, App Passwords* may become necessary for some Facebook linked applications. These applications may require *App Passwords* because they cannot ask for the security codes when logging in to your account, i.e. "David's Xbox". The applications Facebook mentions in their example are Skype, Spotify, Xbox and Jabber. If you do not use many applications linked to your Facebook account, these *App Passwords* may not be necessary.

Recommendation: Only use these passwords for the specific application and purpose named. When creating the password, label them accurately and with sufficient information so you remember where it is used. **NEVER** write these passwords down or share them. These passwords carry the risk of account compromise if someone were to learn them. Change your *App Password* if the site or service linked is compromised. Do not use these to bypass using *Login Approvals* for convenience.

To generate a password, click *Generate App Passwords*.

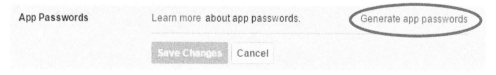

Click *Generate App Passwords* again on the popup.

Generate app passwords

Login Approvals won't always work when you try to access Apps that you log into using Facebook, such as:

- Xbox
- Spotify
- Skype

You can still securely log into these Apps by using an **app password** instead of your Facebook account password. You'll only need to enter your app-specific password once.

Not Now   **Generate App Passwords**

Give your password a name and click *Generate Password.*

Generate app passwords

Type the name of an App you want to approve and we'll automatically generate a password for it:

AppPasswordName|

Cancel   **Generate Password**

The next screen displays the password. Use that password to login to the application required.

Public Key

Public Key allows you to supply an encryption key to Facebook to deliver notifications to you in an encrypted format.

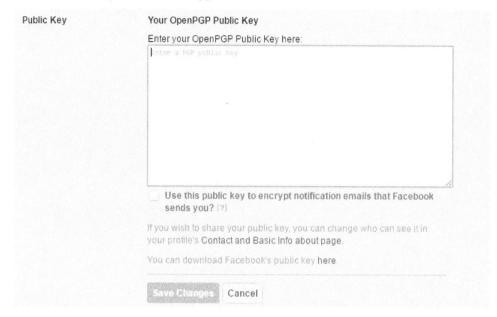

Recommendation: I struggle to find a security reason to use this feature. When enabled, it encrypts the notification emails sent to you by Facebook. I would skip this step, unless you are worried about these emails being intercepted and read by others. My recommendation is to disable Facebook email notifications that reference status updates and activity all together and not worry about using this section.

The setup and use of this section is beyond Facebook security and requires the setup of an email application that can decrypt these messages. If you would like to learn more about this process, please visit the following link. https://goo.gl/sN2MPx (Lifehacker.com).

Your Trusted Contacts

Did you know you can set three to five of your friends to be your most trusted friends who have access to codes to help recover your account if you are unable to login? This feature may also help if you ever lose your authenticator device.

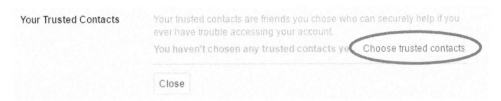

If you would like to choose trusted contacts, click *Choose Trusted Contacts*. The following screen helps explain the trusted contact setting.

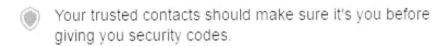

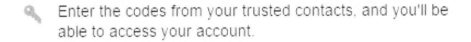

Recommendation: If you frequently are locked out of your account, this feature can help recover your account. It is a unique way to ensure you stay in control of your account and requires both you and your friend is input to generate the unlock code. This may be helpful to set up for a parent or child who may not be technically savvy or may require assistance often.

Choose Trusted Contacts   ✕

Choose 3 to 5 friends that you can call for help if there's ever a
problem with your account. For your security, we'll notify any new
contacts that you add. [?]

Choose friends

Cancel   Confirm

Your friends selected must be your Facebook friend and they will receive a
notification that they are your trusted contact. If you cannot login, you can
use the *Forgot your password* feature on the logon screen. You will select one
of these trusted contacts and Facebook will generate a unique web address
for them to visit. That web address will require them to login to Facebook
and it will generate a code for you to recover your account.

Recognized Devices

Any computer or device (i.e. tablet, smartphone or computer) you have logged in to your account with will show up in the list below.

Recommendation: Check this section occasionally and click remove on any devices you no longer use or anything you don't recognize. If there is a device on the list that you don't recognize, I would suggest removing it and changing your password immediately.

Clicking *Remove* and *Save Changes* will require you to log in the next time you use that removed device. You might need to use this section if you forgot to log off a friend's or public computer.

Where You're Logged In

Similar to the last section of recognized devices, *Where You're Logged In* shows where you are actively logged in to your Facebook account. It will display both the device type, time last accessed and geographic location.

Recommendation: I would also check this section occasionally and end any activity you do not recognize. After activating *Login Approvals,* it is unlikely you will see any unusual activity. If see any strange activity here, I would suggest clicking *End All Activity* and changing your password. Strange activity is sessions shown on devices you do not own (iPhone when you only have Android) or from *Locations* you do not recognize.

Click *End Activity* and your Facebook account will be logged out on the device shown.

Profile Picture Login

This option allows you to click on your profile picture instead of typing a password next time you log in from this browser.

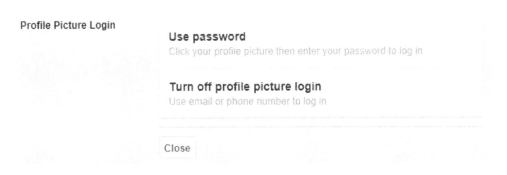

Recommendation: To me, this seems like the opposite of a security feature. It allows you to save your login credentials to the specific computer and browser and lets you click your profile picture to log on, even after 'logging out'.

If you did click *Turn On*, the options change to the next screen shot. It allows you to require your password even when clicking your picture or turn off the option.

Profile Picture Login

Use password
Click your profile picture then enter your password to log in

Turn off profile picture login
Use email or phone number to log in

Close

Legacy Contact

You can choose a Facebook friend to have limited access to some memorial features of your account after you pass away.

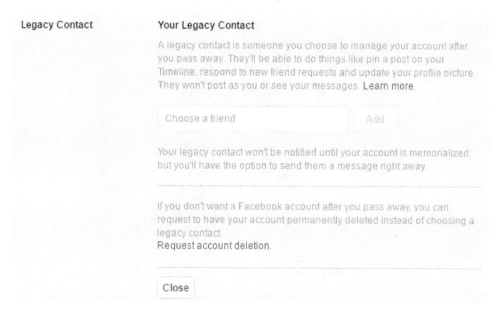

The options are straight forward, set a Facebook friend to be able to pin a memorial post on your account or request your account be deleted after you pass away. Type your friend or family member name in the box, select their account and click *Add*.

Message David About Being Your Legacy Contact

You can use this message to let David know that you chose him, or edit it if you'd like. You also might want to talk in person.

To   David Lyon

Message   Hi David, Facebook now lets people choose a legacy contact to manage their account if something happens to them: https://www.facebook.com/help/1568013990080948

Since you know me well and I trust you, I chose you. Please let me know if you want to talk about this.

Not Now   **Send**

If you would rather have your account deleted, select *Request account deletion*.

This will remove your legacy contact.

Please confirm that you want your account deleted after your death. Once someone lets us know that you passed away, all of your info, photos and posts will be permanently removed from Facebook and no one will be able to see your profile again.

Learn More   Cancel   **Delete After Death**

Recommendation: This is a personal decision, but I do not see a reason to avoid having a legacy contact from a security standpoint. The legacy contact cannot login to your account and cannot access personal information or your messages.

Deactivate Your Account

Deactivate your account disables your account.

Deactivate Your Account

Deactivating your account will disable your profile and remove your n
and photo from most things you've shared on Facebook. Some
information may still be visible to others, such as your name in their
friends list and messages you sent. Learn more.

Deactivate your account.

Close

Recommendation: Unfortunately, Facebook makes it impossible to delete an account. Even if you deactivate your account; you can log back in and POOF, your account is back. If you are certain you want to deactivate your account, I would recommend changing your password to one that is randomly generated and long (20+ characters in length) to ensure hackers can't access your information. If a hacker were to access your account after it's been deactivated, they'd have access to all your information, friends and messages just like your account was active.

 Want to generate a super strong password for this purpose? Use this password generator: https://goo.gl/wnliZa (GRC.com)

Privacy Settings and Security

Congratulations, you have finished securing your account! Now it is time to lock down who can see your profile and your information contained within. Your Facebook profile is a goldmine of social information about you, your friends and your family. If your profile information is posted publicly, everyone can view your Facebook page and use this information for devious purposes.

In the military, this information about you could be classified as OPSEC, or Operations Security. OPSEC is the process of protecting smaller bits of information that could be grouped together to give the bigger picture. You might think it's a stretch to consider personal information on Facebook this way, but imagine this situation:

John posts publicly on Facebook weekly. The topic of these posts include pictures of his friends at his home watching sports, updates when he visits his favorite restaurants and pictures from his vacation. When updating his status, he also checks in to local businesses he visits. He also creates a place on Facebook based on his home and calls it "John's House". John plans a vacation and posts how excited he is prior to leaving. While on vacation, he posts daily updates that get lots of likes and shares from his friends. One person viewing these posts notices that John is not in the country and breaks into his house.

How did this thief know to rob John? John's home, which is a Facebook check-in location, allows the thief to know John's address. The thief also can scope out John's house from the pictures of his friends watching sports and sees a flat screen TV and laptop that would look great in the thief's living room. The thief also knows John is going to be gone for another week and has plenty of time to make sure the coast is clear at John's house. This is an example of OPSEC as each of these pieces of information can be built upon to create a bigger picture and puts a big target on John's home.

 https://goo.gl/Ux5aSo (ZDNet.com, 2011) This article and infographic states 80% of home thieves interviewed checked Facebook, Twitter and Google Street view before breaking in.

It's not just hackers and thieves that may be viewing your public Facebook profile. Potential employers may also be viewing Facebook profiles and deciding whether to hire based on the activity. That picture your John has of him at the bar looking intoxicated may hamper his job hunting prospects.

i https://goo.gl/WfOpA4 (ScienceDaily.com, 2016) Your job application will likely get you looked up on Facebook and your profile picture alone may decide whether you get a call back.

i https://goo.gl/T4eLQo (Careerbuilder.com, 2016) 60% of employers screen with social media.

How do we protect you from these situations? Our first mission is to protect your profile from the public's view and then narrow and refine your friend list's view

Setting Up Friend Lists

There is one prerequisite I would like to cover before we continue to the profile information lockdown. To avoid double work on setting your profile protection, I would advise we group your current friends into separate lists first. Facebook makes things complicated for us by calling your total list of friends your 'Friends List'; however, you can create groups of friends within your Facebook, these are 'Friend Lists'. Let us make it a little easier to differentiate, for our purposes, by calling these groups of friends just *Lists*. *Lists* is Facebook's way of organizing friends in to security groups that allow you to control what each group can see of your profile and posts.

To show this concept visually, imagine you have 200 friends and want to group them by family, close friends and everyone else.

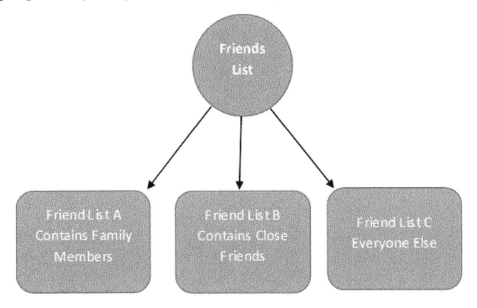

Grouping your Facebook friends this way allows you to post items to your Timeline that only *List A, List B, List C* or any combination of those *Lists* can view. The Timeline is the location where all your activity, and activity you are tagged in, displays in your profile.

In this section, we will set up at least one of these separate *Lists* for your friends. On my own Facebook account, I leave my close friends in the standard Facebook friends list and place the rest in one of these separate *Lists*. It's my recommendation that you create these *Lists* to only allow your posts to be seen by a core group of your friends.

Just as a reminder, this *List* is created to either limit or grant viewing access to your posts and profile information. It is probably easiest to create a *List* to block specific groups of friends from viewing your profile and posts. **A single blocking List is the example we will be using going forward.**

 Keep in mind, this section is optional. Although, if you do not set up these Friend Lists, your changes to your privacy settings will apply to all friends on your Facebook account.

For instance, when creating a new post on your Timeline, you will not be able to pick or narrow your audience; all your friends will see the post.

Return to the main Facebook page by clicking the Facebook icon in the top left. On the left column of the main Facebook page, click on the *Friend Lists* option.

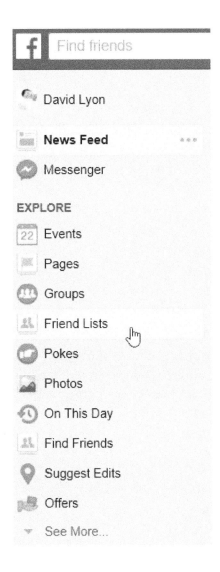

The following screen will load and show you the current lists in your profile. Since we will be making a list to protect your information, click *Create List*.

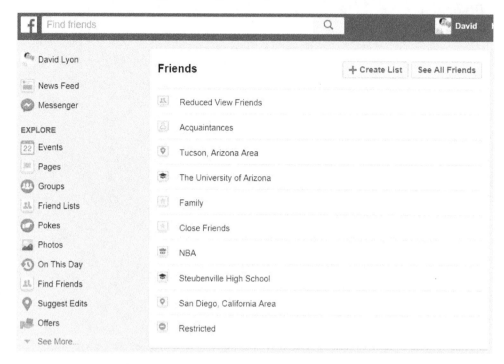

The following screen will pop-up and allow you to create your *List*. Create a name for the *List* and add a friend you would like to manage. Do not worry about adding everyone at once; we can come back later to add more friends.

You can create a *List* for every type of security group you would like, so repeat the steps above to create more *Lists* if you would like. For instance, if you would like a group of friends who can't see your status updates, and another blocked from your profile information, create separate *Lists* for those people.

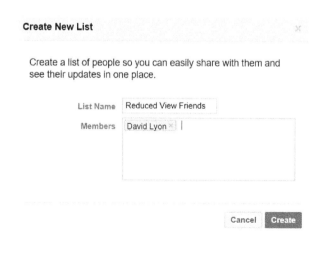

After you create the *List,* you will be taken to a page that displays any posts from those friends and where you can post only to that group.

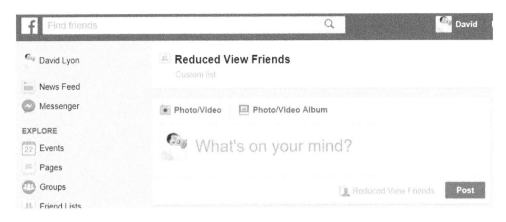

As you can see, it shows *Reduced View Friends* next to the *Post* button. This is the audience of the message if I updated my status. Only people in the *Reduced View Friends* group will see this post.

To add members, rename or delete this *List,* the *Friend Lists* selection from the left column.

Then click on the name of the *List.*

In the top right corner, click *Manage List.*

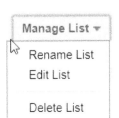

Clicking on *Edit List* will allow you to add more members.

Change the drop down from *On This List to Friends* to show all your friends that can be added to the *List*. Go ahead and select the friends you would like to add to the *List* and then click *Finish* in the bottom right.

Now that you have created a *List*, we will modify your profile security.

Edit Reduced View Friends

On This List ▾

Search...

David Lyon

Hide Profile Information

Remember our friend John? Let us imagine he also keeps all his profile information public and up-to-date. His workplace, education, contact information, towns he has lived in are all stored on Facebook. With this information and some searches on Google, a thief or stalker could easily find where John works, his hours, when he is not at home, and maybe his home address and phone number.

Our first goal is to hide your profile information from the public and any *Lists* that you set up in the previous section. We do not want you to be like John. By default, Facebook sets a lot of your profile information as publicly viewable. For your security, there is no reason anyone who is not a friend should be able to view any of your profile information.

From the Facebook Timeline, click on your first name next to your small profile picture.

This will take you to your profile information page. Since this is a profile I set up for the purpose of this book, I loaded it with a bunch of fake information and left the security settings at default. Let us change those settings now.

Next to your profile picture, click *About*. I hope you enjoy my silly fake profile picture.

Your Timeline page will change and Facebook will show you the overview of your profile information. Inside each section, there are privacy settings that should be changed.

Click on *Work and Education.*

Your stored work and education information will be shown on the next page. When you mouse over any stored information, a small icon and the *Options* menu will appear. In my case, the globe appears because the stored information of being an NBA Basketball Player is shown publicly. Clicking on *Options* will allow you to see the date when you entered this item, edit the dates or information or delete the information all together. To change the privacy setting on that item, click on the globe icon shown. Your icon may be different depending on your current security setting.

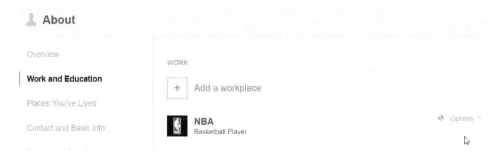

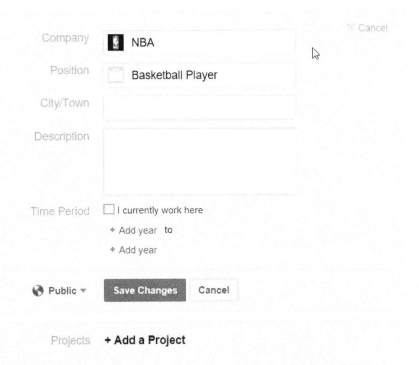

The screen above will appear for the profile information. Notice next to *Save Changes,* the *Public* and globe icon appear again, click the down arrow.

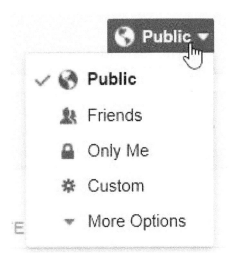

The selections right will appear and allow you to change who can view the information in this section. *Public* is the default, but let us change it to *Custom* since we created the Reduced View Friends *List* earlier. If you would like even more security, changing this setting to *Only Me* will only allow you to view the information.

Custom Privacy

Share with

These people or lists | Friends ×

Friends of tagged

Anyone tagged will be able to see this post.

Don't share with

These people or lists | Reduced View Friends ×

Anyone you include here or have on your restricted list won't be able to see this post unless you tag them. We don't let people know when you choose to not share something with them.

Cancel **Save Changes**

This *Custom Privacy* window will appear and I recommend getting to know the settings here as they reoccur often throughout Facebook's security settings. The top box is the *Lists* of friends who can see this profile information while the bottom is the Lists that cannot. How it is set above, my *List* called "Friends", which is my whole Friends List, minus those in the "Reduced View Friends" list can see the information. I recommend also unchecking the *Friends of Tagged* as it opens up your information and posts to the friends of your friends who would be tagged in any post. For instance, if you tagged your friend John in your status update, all his friends would also be able to view that post. Do you know and trust all of John's friends?

After you have clicked *Saved Changes* the globe turns in to a gear and *Custom*.

Click *Save Changes* again to save the security settings for that profile information section. While changing your security settings, Facebook may recommend adding friends who may be coworkers or students at the same school. I suggest ignoring these by selecting *Cancel*.

Now that you have successfully changed the security setting on the About section of your profile, continue down all the options on the left column. Each piece of information you have stored in your profile has the same privacy icon and settings.

Work and Education

Places You've Lived

Contact and Basic Info

Family and Relationships

Details About You

Life Events

Visit each section and make sure all your information is at minimum set to *Friends* and not *Public*.

Public is denoted by the globe above.

     Options

Friends is shown with the two people's heads above.

I still recommend the *Custom* setting so you can pick and choose which Facebook friends should see your profile information.

After you've completed setting your privacy on all your profile information, click on your *Friends* tab from your profile.

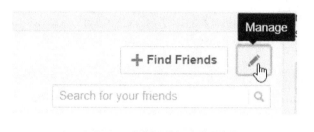

Then click on the pencil icon just below the navigation bar shown below.

Click *Edit Privacy*.

The following two options will appear.

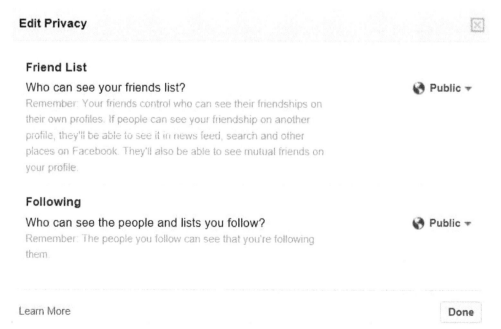

Edit Privacy

Friend List

Who can see your friends list?

🌐 Public ▾

Remember: Your friends control who can see their friendships on their own profiles. If people can see your friendship on another profile, they'll be able to see it in news feed, search and other places on Facebook. They'll also be able to see mutual friends on your profile.

Following

Who can see the people and lists you follow?

🌐 Public ▾

Remember: The people you follow can see that you're following them.

Learn More

Done

I recommend changing these sections so they are not public. Reducing the view of this information may not have stopped John from being robbed, but your friends list could be OPSEC when combined with other information. The best security practice would be to lock it down to *Only Me*, but *Friends* or *Custom* with the *Reduced View Friends List* would also be a good choice. Do your current friends really need to be able to see with whom you are friends? Probably not, that is why I use *Only Me*.

After hiding your Friends List, we will continue to your photos. Click on the *Photos* section of the menu bar.

Click on *Albums*.

Assuming you have uploaded pictures in the past, you should have some albums listed. Since I created this account for the purpose of this tutorial, I have only one album. Your cover and profile photos always get their own albums. The current cover photo and profile picture are always set public and cannot be changed.

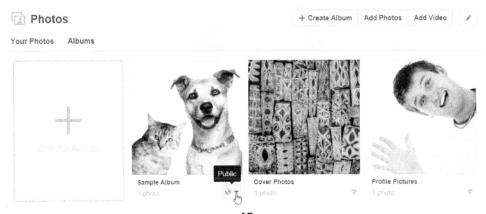

Notice the picture of my Sample Album, there is the globe again with the drop down menu to change the security setting. Go through any existing albums you have and change the settings to your desired privacy level.

The menu is slightly different from those previously, but states the same information. I went ahead and changed these pictures to show to *Friends*.

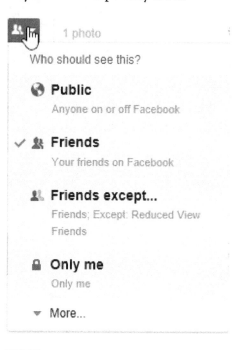

If you would like to continue the previous security settings using the *Lists* we created earlier, click *Friends except....*

A slightly different menu will appear as shown in the next screen shot. Select the List with the red caution sign that you would like to not share with.

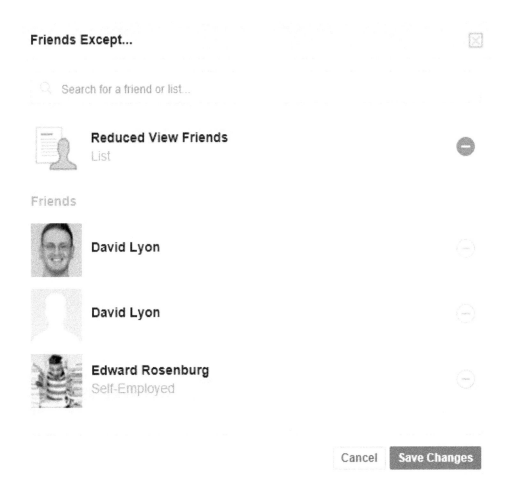

Click *Save Changes.*

Test Your Profile View

You have now completed changing all the security settings on your profile information. To test the view of your profile from another point of view, click on the ⋯ icon next to *View Activity Log*.

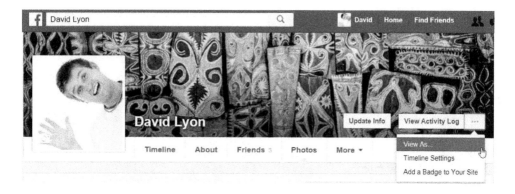

Then click *View As....*

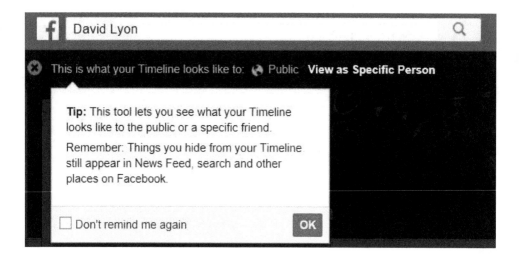

Facebook shows you this prompt the first time you use this feature. It explains that you are viewing your profile as the selected person or group. Click *OK* and preview your profile information.

At the top of the page in the black bar it mentions Facebook is displaying your profile as Public. This is a good view to start with, as people publicly should not be able to view any information. If you see information displayed on your profile while in Public view, I would return to the previous steps and change the security setting on that information.

As a reminder, your profile picture and cover photo cannot be made private. It will always be public.

Once you are satisfied with the Public view, change your display to one of the friends that you added to the *Reduced View Friends List.*

Click on *View as a Specific Person.*

Then type in a friend from the *Reduced View Friends List.*

Scroll through your profile information and make sure you are satisfied with the *Reduced View Friends* view as well.

Your current profile information is now protected from the *Lists* that we set up earlier. Remember if you add or make any changes to your profile in the future; set the privacy on that information as well.

Clean Up Past Timeline Posts

Past posts on your Facebook Timeline are also treasure troves of information for potential bad guys. Take an honest look back through your Timeline by clicking on your name on the top blue Facebook bar.

Our friend John had posted a picture of his mother's birthday party some years ago. He had forgotten it even existed as it had moved further down his Timeline, but a hacker found it as it was posted publicly. Somewhere in the comments, someone referenced his mom by her maiden name, which provided that hacker with the answer to John's online security question for his bank. While this story may be a stretch of imagination, information from your profile can be used in this way.

Scroll down and let the page load multiple times as your travel back in time on your Facebook Timeline. You may have some great memories located in your Timeline, but do you really want to continue sharing all that information with all your friends or maybe even publicly?

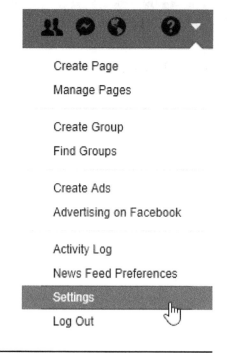

It is my recommendation that we hide all older information in your Timeline completely and use the *Lists* that we created earlier to target all future posts.

Facebook makes it easy to hide all older information, so let us start with that first.

From any Facebook page, click on the down arrow icon in the top right. Then click on *Settings*.

Create Page

Manage Pages

Create Group

Find Groups

Create Ads

Advertising on Facebook

Activity Log

News Feed Preferences

Settings

Log Out

This should take you to the *General* menu. Click on the *Privacy* menu on the left.

From this screen, there is section called *Who can see my stuff?* Click on *Limit Past Posts* next to the description *Limit the audience for posts you've shared with friends of friends or Public.*

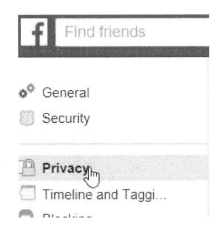

 This process cannot be reversed and only changes those Timeline posts shown as *Public* or *Friends of Friends* to the *Friends* setting. If you want to revert to previous settings, it must be done manually.

Clicking the *Limit Past Posts* will expand this section to explain in detail what occurs when this process is run. It only locks down older Timeline posts to the security setting of *Friends* and is much easier than changing each post individually. Facebook does not provide a time of what it considers 'old'.

Despite this warning, I recommend you run this tool to ensure you have no old posts that may be shared publicly. This tool does not remove the posts or remove your Friend's ability to view them. It only changes Timeline posts that may be shared publicly.

After clicking *Limit Old Posts*, Facebook warns you again. Click *Confirm*.

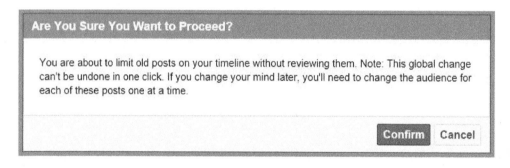

This may be enough for some people, but I would recommend also manually searching your Timeline for sensitive information and deleting those posts (or limiting the audience to *Only Me*). Information you may want to look for include your phone number, address, location information that might show where you live or pictures of any of this information.

Click again on your name to view your Timeline.

Scroll down and keep an eye on the right side of the page to view your Timeline posts. Two sample posts are shown below.

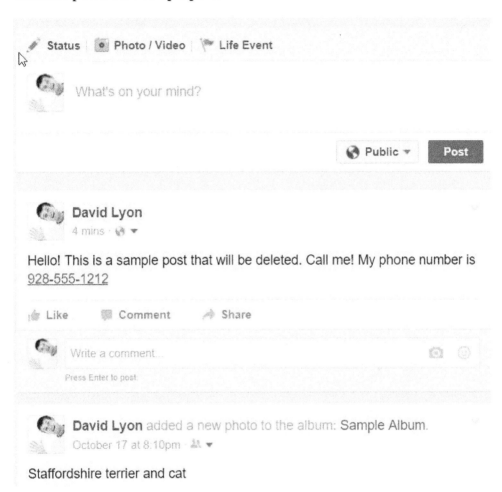

Notice next to the time posted and my name is that globe icon again. Your icon may be different depending on the privacy settings of your posts and if you ran the previous limit audience tool. If you would like to change the security settings on that post, click that icon.

The similar privacy selection screen appears and allows you to change the audience of the post.

Since this post contains my fake phone number, let's delete it instead.

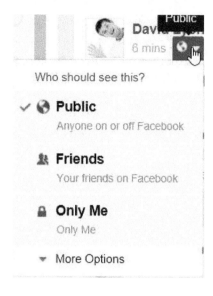

In the top right corner of the post, there is a light blue downwards arrow. Click on that arrow.

There are two options here related to the post security and privacy.

Hide from Timeline will only remove this post from being displayed on your Timeline. The post can still appear in other peoples' Newsfeeds, depending on privacy settings, and possibly your Activity Feed. The Newsfeed is the home page of scrolling information displayed when you log in to Facebook. Activity Feed will be covered later.

If this were something truly sensitive, I would not recommend using the *Hide from Timeline* feature as the post still exists.

Delete is a better option as it removes the post from all locations in Facebook. Imagine John hides a post that contains his phone number but that post has a friend tagged. That friend and all of John's friends' friends can still see that post and any activity related.

This warning appears when you click *Delete*. Select *Delete Post* will completely remove the post from your Timeline.

I, again, strongly recommend reviewing your entire Timeline and deleting any posts that may identify you, where you or family lives, or contains any personal information or pictures that contain specific personal information. This process will take some time if you are active on Facebook or have had an account for a long time.

Now that you have cleaned up your Timeline, it is time to ensure your future posts stay private.

Secure Future Profile Information

When John follows the previous sections, he has removed any old and profile information from the hacker's eyes. However, without securing his future posts, he can still be targeted.

In this section we will ensure all future information you post on Facebook can only be viewed by those you chose.

We will be working again in the privacy menu. From any main Facebook page, click on the down arrow icon in the top right, then click Settings.

This will take you to the *General* menu, click on *Privacy*. We will be changing these settings first.

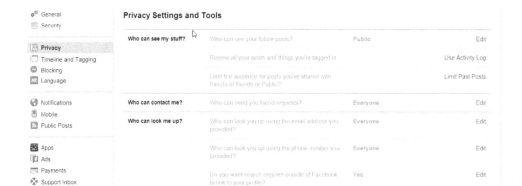

Under the options of *Who can see my stuff* is the *Who can see your future posts?* setting. Notice my setting is currently *Public* which would allow anyone on Facebook to see my posts. Click *Edit*.

Facebook gives a quick explanation of the settings changed here and what it does. This setting will set the default audience of any of your future Facebook posts. You can also change this audience when posting. I'm going to change my future post to exclude the Lists we created earlier. Click on the globe and *Public* dropdown.

Click *More Options.*

Then click *Custom.*

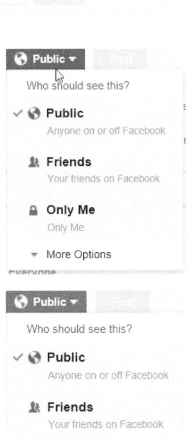

Custom Privacy

✛ Share with

These people or lists | Friends ✕ |

Friends of tagged   ✓

Anyone tagged will be able to see this post.

✕ Don't share with

These people or lists

Anyone you include here or have on your
restricted list won't be able to see this post
unless you tag them. We don't let people know
when you choose to not share something with
them.

Cancel   **Save Changes**

I am going to not share with the group called *Reduced View Friends* that I created earlier and remove the check from *Friends of tagged* to limit the audience. It is my recommendation to limit your audience to as small a group of friends as possible.

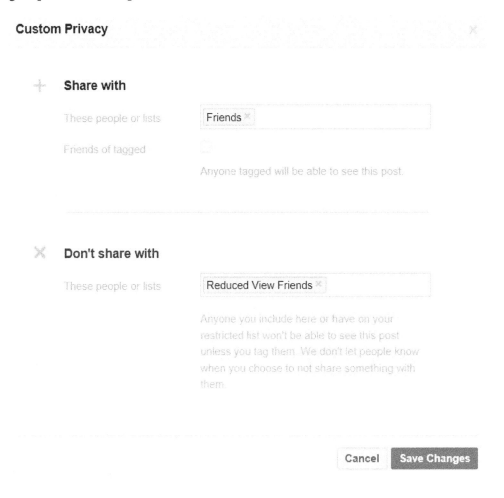

After you are done, click *Save Changes* to return to the previous menu. Facebook gives you this notice reminding you that you can also customize this setting when composing your post.

> **Remember:** This is the same setting you find right where you post, and by changing it here, you've also updated it there.

Skip down to *Who can contact me?* Click *Edit* next to the question *Who can send you friend requests?* Facebook only allows two options, *Everyone* and *Friends of Friends.*

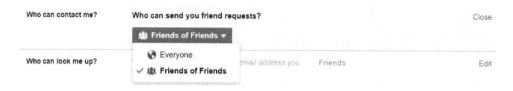

If you often receive friend requests from people outside your *Friends of Friends,* you can leave this option as *Everyone*. Otherwise, I would suggest setting to the *Friends of Friends* option to cut down on friend requests from people you likely don't know.

The next three settings, in the *Who can look me up?* section, are controls on how people can find you on Facebook with information like your email address, phone number or external search engine.

Who can look me up?		
	Who can look you up using the email address you provided?	Friends
	Who can look you up using the phone number you provided?	Friends
	Do you want search engines outside of Facebook to link to your profile?	No

My recommendation for these is to lock it down as securely as possible to the above settings. If someone you do not know was able to acquire your email address or phone number, they would be able to look up your profile very easily. For example, with Everyone set, if you were to submit your resume for a job opening that contained your phone number and email address, they could easily identify which profile is yours just from a simple search.

Click *Edit* next to each line and check the settings in the drop down menu. Again, my recommendation is changing this to *Friends* or at least *Friends of Friends.*

The last option of the group is *Do you want search engines outside of Facebook to link to your profile?* I also recommend turning this option off to keep people from easily using search engines like Google or Bing to find your profile by name. This will reduce the search engine results for your name and make it a little harder for people to search for you to acquire information. Facebook provides the following warning when you turn this option off.

Click *Turn Off.*

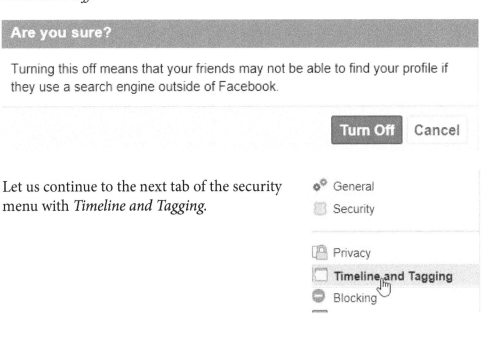

Let us continue to the next tab of the security menu with *Timeline and Tagging.*

This section allows you to control your privacy settings for your personal Timeline and if people can tag you in their posts.

Timeline and Tagging Settings

Who can add things to my Timeline?	Who can post on your Timeline?	Friends	Edit
	Review posts friends tag you in before they appear on your Timeline?	Off	Edit
Who can see things on my Timeline?	Review what other people see on your Timeline		View As
	Who can see posts you've been tagged in on your Timeline?	Friends	Edit
	Who can see what others post on your Timeline?	Friends	Edit
How can I manage tags people add and tagging suggestions?	Review tags people add to your own posts before the tags appear on Facebook?	Off	Edit
	When you're tagged in a post, who do you want to add to the audience if they aren't already in it?	Friends	Edit
	Who sees tag suggestions when photos that look like you are uploaded?	Friends	Edit

Starting with *Who can post on your Timeline?*, click *Edit* and modify your selection. Facebook only allows two settings for this, *Friends* and *Only Me*. If you do not want your friends posting on your Timeline, change it to *Only Me*.

Review posts friends tag you in before they appear on your Timeline? is an important setting that allows you to review any tags before your friends can see them. It is my recommendation to turn this setting on, which is covered next.

John may be getting smarter now about his Facebook security, but imagine he is out of town and his friend posts to their own Timeline, "Wish you were here! Hope you're enjoying your vacation!" and tags John. Instantly, that post appears on your Timeline and now his friends know he is not home. You cannot change your friends' security practices, but Facebook allows you to control their actions on your profile.

Changing this setting to *Enabled* will make it so you receive a notification when you are tagged to approve that tag.

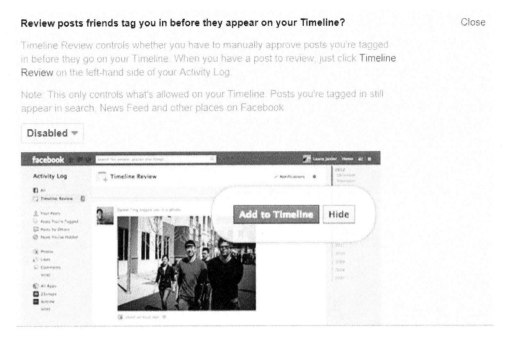

Review posts friends tag you in before they appear on your Timeline?   Close

Timeline Review controls whether you have to manually approve posts you're tagged in before they go on your Timeline. When you have a post to review, just click Timeline Review on the left-hand side of your Activity Log.

Note: This only controls what's allowed on your Timeline. Posts you're tagged in still appear in search, News Feed and other places on Facebook

Disabled ▾

The next section is *Who can see things on my Timeline?* The first setting is a review of the *View As* feature we covered when changing your profile security settings in the last chapter.

The next two settings in this section are listed below.

Who can see posts you've been tagged in on your Timeline?   **Friends**   Edit

Who can see what others post on your Timeline?   **Friends**   Edit

Who can see posts you've been tagged in on your Timeline? is an option to change the audience of posts added to your Timeline by tags.
Who can see what others post on your Timeline? will change the audience of all other posts to your Timeline.

Both of these settings allow more customization than some of the previous options.

Clicking *Edit* allows you to use the *Lists* of friends we set up earlier. I recommend using the *Custom* setting again and excluding the *List* of blocked friends.

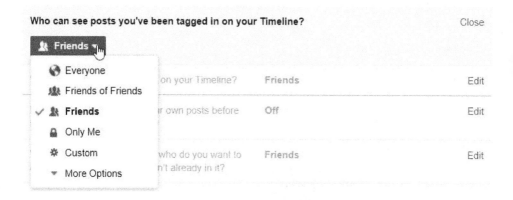

The final group of settings called *How can I manage tags people add and tagging suggestions?* is shown below. Tags are names of places added to posts that link it to a profile or location.

How can I manage tags people add and tagging suggestions?	Review tags people add to your own posts before the tags appear on Facebook?	Off	Edit
	When you're tagged in a post, who do you want to add to the audience if they aren't already in it?	Friends	Edit
	Who sees tag suggestions when photos that look like you are uploaded?	Friends	Edit

Click *Edit* next to *Review tags people add to your own posts before the tags appear on Facebook?* lets you control who can add tags to your posts. An example is shown in the screen shot below.

Review tags people add to your own posts before the tags appear on Facebook?

Turn on Tag Review to review tags friends add to your content before they appear on Facebook. When someone who you're not friends with adds a tag to one of your posts you'll always be asked to review it.

Remember: When you approve a tag, the person tagged and their friends may be able to see your post.

Disabled ▼

I recommend *Enabling* this option to help limit the audience of your posts. Any of your friends could tag anyone else and any friend of that tagged person becomes the audience of your post.

The next setting is: *When you're tagged in a post, who do you want to add to the audience if they aren't already in it?*

When you're tagged in a post, who do you want to add to the audience if they aren't already in it?   Close

👥 Friends ▼

Do you want all your friends to see a post when you are tagged? I would recommend no, or at minimum changing this to *Custom* and excluding the *Reduced View List*. I would suggest setting this option to *Only Me* to prevent the unauthorized tagging situations I mentioned earlier where your friend mentions you are on vacation.

Finally, the last option in this section: *Who sees tag suggestions when photos that look like you are uploaded?*

There is little security risk for this setting as it only allows *Friends* and *No One*. If you'd like your friends to be able to tag you quickly in photos and receive these suggestions, go ahead and leave it as *Friends*.

The next section is *Blocking*. Why would you block someone over removing him or her as a friend? You can still view their profile, but they will not be able to view yours.

John may start using the Block feature to allow him to monitor some acquaintances, but remove them from being able to see and share his posts and information.

This section is rather self-explanatory, but there is one option I would like to point out. Click on *Blocking* in the left column.

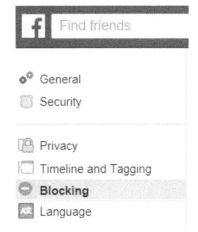

The very first option is *Restricted List.*

Restricted List	When you add a friend to your Restricted List, they won't see posts on Facebook that you share only to Friends. They may still see things you share to Public or on a mutual friend's Timeline, and posts they're tagged in. Facebook doesn't notify your friends when you add them to your Restricted List. Learn more	Edit List

By clicking *Edit List,* you can add any of your friends to a limited security group, which is very similar to the *Lists* idea presented earlier. This List is special because it removes any friend added from the sharing granted by the *Friends* group. For example, if you create a post that's set to share with Friends and you add Bob to this *Restricted List,* Bob won't see that post.

The rest of the *Blocking* settings are important to understand and review about but are self-explanatory and have good descriptions from Facebook. Review these settings and add any people, applications or pages you want to block.

Miscellaneous Security Settings

Your past profile information and all posts in the future are now secure. There are only a few more settings that should be reviewed to protect your profile and information.

From any Facebook page, click on the down arrow icon and go to *Settings*.

Create Page
Manage Pages

Create Group
Find Groups

Create Ads
Advertising on Facebook

Activity Log
News Feed Preferences
Settings
Log Out

General
Security

Privacy
Timeline and Tagging
Blocking
Language

Notifications
Mobile
Public Posts

Apps
Ads
Payments
Support Inbox
Videos

From the left column, click on *Public Posts*.

At this time, any Friend is allowed to follow your public posts. If you post publicly and want anyone to be able to follow your posts, you will want to modify the first setting on this page.

Who Can Follow Me — Followers see your posts in News Feed. Friends follow your posts by default, but you can also allow people who are not your friends to follow your public posts. Use this setting to choose who can follow you.

Each time you post, you choose which audience you want to share with.

Learn more.

Friends ▾

The two options are *Friends* and *Public*. If you never plan on posting publicly, I would advise changing this to *Friends* to limit who can follow your profile.

The section below this setting allows you to modify the behavior and security of your public posts.

Public Post Comments	Who can comment on your public posts? Public	Edit
Public Post Notifications	Get notifications from Public	Edit
Public Profile Info	Who can like or comment on your public profile pictures and other profile info? Friends	Edit
Comment Ranking	Comment ranking is Off	Edit
Username		Edit
Twitter	Connect a Twitter account	Edit

Want to know what followers can see? View your public timeline.

While I don't recommend ever posting publicly from your personal Facebook profile, I would recommend modifying these settings to the most private setting to limit the audience of potential accidental public posting. Click *Edit* next to each section below in italics below.

Public Post Comments sets who can post on your public posts. The three settings allowed are *Public, Friends of Friends* and *Friends*.

Public Post Notifications lets you know when someone from the specified audience follows your profile. For instance, if it's set for *Public,* Facebook will notify you when someone who is not your Friend follows your profile. The three available options are *Public, Friends of Friends* and *Nobody*.

Public Profile Info lets you limit the commenting and liking of your always public profile information. I would recommend setting this to *Friends* so strangers cannot comment on your profile picture, cover photos or your bio. The three options here are *Public, Friends of Friends* and *Friends.*

Comment Ranking will only change the sorting of comments on your public posts. Most liked posts will show up at the top of the comments section.

Username allows you to select a short web address to link to your Facebook profile.

Another setting that is overlooked but security relevant is in the *Apps* section. Click on *Apps* in the left column.

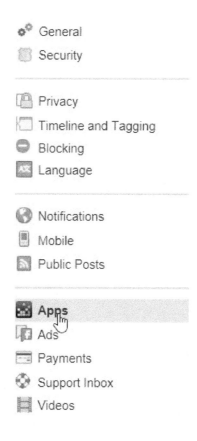

There are four settings on this page that can be changed to provide more privacy for your profile.

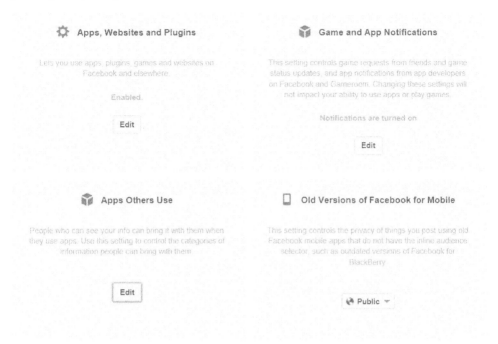

Starting in the top left with *Apps, Websites and Plugins,* this setting allows your Facebook profile and information to be used to play games and log in to other websites. If you never use your Facebook profile for games or logging in to other locations, you can turn this off. With it off though, you will not be able to use these functions.

Bottom left setting, *Apps Others Use,* allows you to limit what information your Friends share with Applications about you. I would recommend clicking Edit and unchecking all the boxes from the popup.

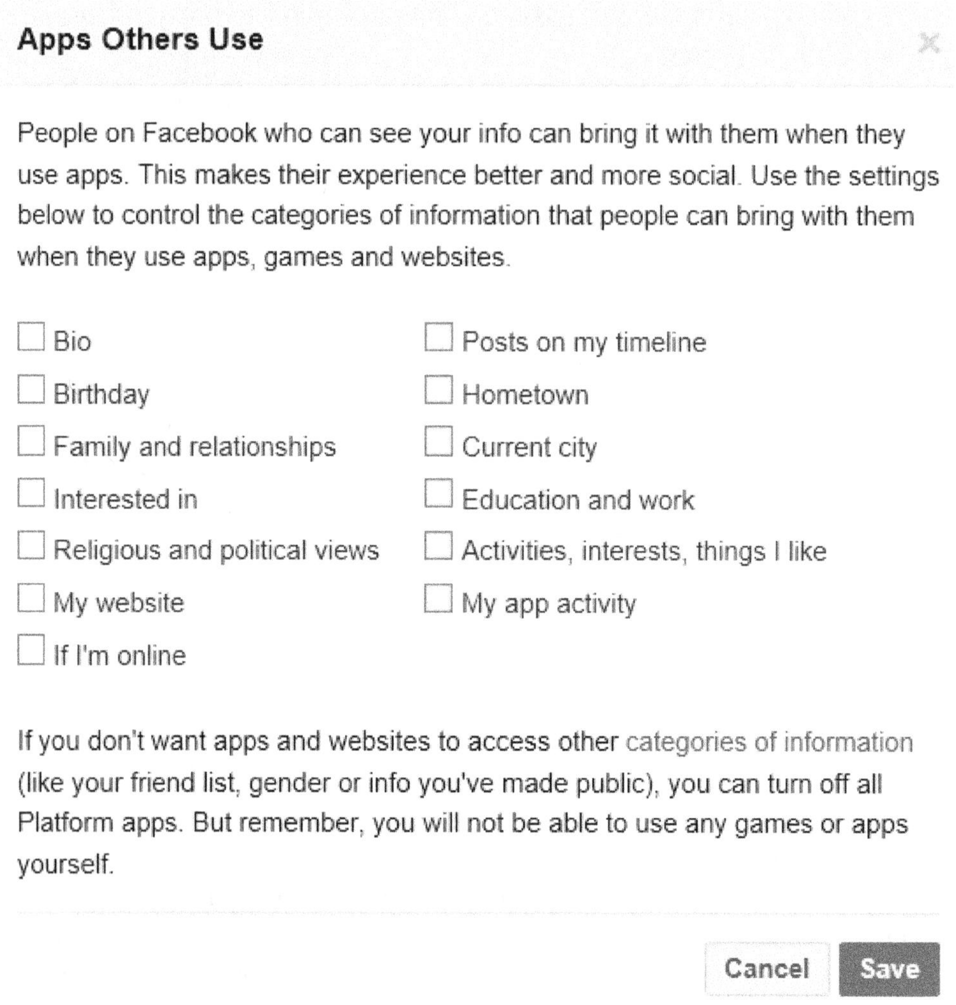

Apps Others Use

People on Facebook who can see your info can bring it with them when they use apps. This makes their experience better and more social. Use the settings below to control the categories of information that people can bring with them when they use apps, games and websites.

☐ Bio
☐ Birthday
☐ Family and relationships
☐ Interested in
☐ Religious and political views
☐ My website
☐ If I'm online

☐ Posts on my timeline
☐ Hometown
☐ Current city
☐ Education and work
☐ Activities, interests, things I like
☐ My app activity

If you don't want apps and websites to access other categories of information (like your friend list, gender or info you've made public), you can turn off all Platform apps. But remember, you will not be able to use any games or apps yourself.

Cancel Save

There is no reason your Friends should be able to share this information about you with third parties or applications they use. This information could be shared with games they play on Facebook and could be used for marketing purposes or worse.

Top right setting, *Game and App Notifications,* allows you to disable annoying notifications from your friends and games you may play on Facebook. No, I do not want to play silly Facebook games all day, and no, I do not want to plant crops for you. I recommend turning off these notifications if you do not want to see them. Screen shot below shows they have already been turned off, please click *Turn Off* if yours are currently On.

Game and App Notifications

Game and app notifications are turned off

Turning on game and app notifications will re-enable those notifications on
Facebook and Gameroom based on your previous settings.

Cancel   **Turn On**

Finally, the bottom right setting, *Old Versions of Facebook for Mobile,* allows
you to change the default posting setting for old versions of Facebook. For
instance, if you use a Palm or Blackberry device to post to Facebook, you
would want to change this setting. Whether you have an old device or not, I
would recommend changing this setting to your usual default audience.

For my setting, I would choose *Custom* then add *Friends* and limit *Reduced
View Friends.*

Our last security section is *Ads.* Click on that section of the left column. What Facebook does with Ads on and off their page can be creepy. Have you ever seen an ad for something that you were just looking at on Amazon or shopping for online? Modifying these settings will reduce those ads.

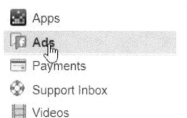

There are only four settings in this section.
The first is *Ads based on my use of websites and apps.*

Ads based on my use of websites and apps	Can you see online interest-based ads from Facebook?	Yes	Edit
	Your status is based on your device settings and any choices you have made with the Digital Advertising Alliance ❶		

This setting allows Facebook to track your profile across any website with Facebook advertising and Like buttons installed. They will use this activity to target ads to your profile. I would recommend changing this setting by clicking *Edit* then using the drop down to select *Off.*

Next is *Ads on apps and website off of the Facebook Companies.*

Ads on apps and websites off of the Facebook Companies	Can your Facebook ad preferences be used to show you ads on apps and websites off of the Facebook Companies?	Yes	Edit

This is similar to the previous setting. It allows Facebook to tailor ads, outside of Facebook, based on your behavior. Again, I recommend changing this setting to *No* by clicking Edit and changing the drop down to *No.*

74

The next setting is *Ads with my Social Actions.*

Ads with my social actions   Who can see your social actions paired with ads?   Only my friends   Edit

When this is enabled, it lets Facebook show your name next to ads of
Facebook pages that you Like. An
example from their page is shown
below where it shows "David Lyon
likes this". I would also recommend
disabling this setting by clicking *Edit*
and using the drop down to select *No
One.*

The final setting is *Ads based on my preferences.* Clicking *Edit* will bring up the description of this section and what control you have.

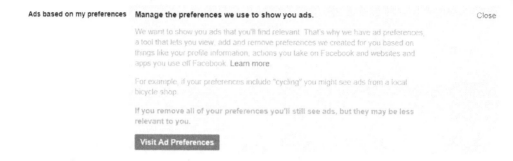

Clicking *Visit Ad Preferences* will bring you to a page that shows you all the information advertisers on Facebook can use to target you directly. There are two major sections of this page, *Interests* and *Advertisers.*

Interests are the Facebook activities or groups that show your interest in a subject that will be shared with advertisers.

Advertisers is a listing of companies and people who have access to your advertising profile which may include contact information.

Advertisers

Advertisers with your contact info   Advertisers whose website or app you've used

Review advertisers whose ads you may be seeing currently because you're on their customer list. Learn more.

Amazon.co.uk

Click through the tabs of the *Interests* section and remove any interests you do not want as a target for advertising. In the above picture, it shows how to mouse over an interest and click the *X* to remove the interest. Apparently I enjoy sleeping, BMWs, gyms and Budweiser.

These settings allow Facebook to tailor their ads to what they believe are your preferences. Removing these preferences, especially the Advertisers, allows you a bit more anonymity on Facebook from advertisers. It's my recommendation to remove all preferences.

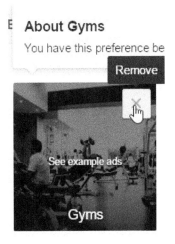

About Gyms

You have this preference be

Remove

See example ads

Gyms

Thank you

Thank you for purchasing this book from the **Keeping You Secure** series. I hope this guide has helped you feel more secure in the use of Facebook. Your profile on Facebook should now be much more private and secure.

If there are any topics you would like to see a book on in the future, please contact me through Amazon or on Goodreads. I hope to hear from you and am always looking for recommendations for the next book in the series.

This is the second book in the series, with the first being *Android – Keeping You Secure.*

www.ingramcontent.com/pod-product-compliance
Lightning Source LLC
LaVergne TN
LVHW052310060326
832902LV00021B/3805